THE
CONGRESS

Illustrated by Leonard Everett Fisher

WILLIAM MORROW AND COMPANY
New York

1963

THE
CONGRESS

2099

BY
GERALD W. JOHNSON

TO

GERALD VAN DEN HONERT

Contents

CHAPTER ONE
How Congress Works
PAGE 13

CHAPTER TWO
The Beginnings of Congress
PAGE 51

CHAPTER THREE
Check and Balance
PAGE 70

List of Speakers
of the House of Representatives
PAGE 119

List of Vice-Presidents
of the United States
PAGE 121

List of Standing Committees
of the Senate and House of Representatives
PAGE 123

Index
PAGE 125

Illustrations

Joint session of Congress in the newly decorated chamber of the House of Representatives 16-17

Congressional hearing held by a subcommittee 22-23

Registration table and voting booth at the polls 30-31

Gerrymander 34

President Theodore Roosevelt signing a bill in the presence of Congressional dignitaries 40-41

George Washington, James Madison, Benjamin Franklin, and Alexander Hamilton 52-53

Unfinished Capitol building just before Lincoln's first inauguration 60-61

French Revolution 72-73

Henry Clay speaking in the old Senate chamber 82-83

Civil War 90-91

Campaign in first direct election of Federal Senators, 1912 100-101

Senate investigation 112-113

THE
CONGRESS

How Congress Works

THE SECOND THING sure to catch your eye when you visit the city of Washington is the Capitol. The first is the monument to George Washington. You can't miss that, because it is the tallest structure in the city, five hundred and fifty-five feet. The Capitol is only two hundred and eighty-seven feet tall, but it spreads over three and a half acres, and it sits on top of a bluff overlooking that part of the city where most of the important government buildings are.

Because it is huge, high, and white you can hardly avoid looking at the Capitol, but to understand it you must have some idea of what it is for, and why it is there. Looking up the word in the dictionary doesn't help much. The dictionary says that the Capitol in Washington is the building in which the sessions of Congress are held. But what is Congress?

The dictionary says that Congress is the legislative branch of the American government. But what is legislative?

The dictionary says that legislative means law-making. But what is law?

In answer to that question the dictionary says a great deal and much of it is hard to understand. It is no wonder, then, that many young people, and some old ones, give the wrong answer. And if you don't understand what law is, you will not understand legislative, and if you don't understand legislative, you will not understand Congress, and if you don't understand Congress, you will not understand the government, and if you don't understand the government, how can you be a first-rate American citizen?

Everyone knows that if we don't obey the law we may be punished. From that, many of us get the idea that the main purpose of the law is to make us do what someone else wants us to do, instead of doing as we please. The law does say that if a man turns into a robber he shall be locked up in jail, but its main purpose is not to get anybody locked up; it is to give honest people a chance to go about their business without being robbed.

The law is a set of rules by which great numbers of people can live close together without getting in each other's way, or trampling each other, or constantly fighting each other.

In the United States there were, when this book was being written, about a hundred and eighty-five million people. This is a number so great that nobody can have more than a dim idea of what it means. It is plain enough, however, that this many people, if they are to go about their affairs easily and safely, will require a very large number of rules, that is to say, laws.

More than that, the things that we use and among which we live are constantly changing, which means that the laws must be constantly changed. George Washington never drove an automobile because the automobile had not been invented when he lived, so there was then no need of a law requiring him to stop when a traffic light turns red. There was no need of a traffic light then, so it had not been invented, either. But today if drivers did not stop at a red light, there would be collisions at every corner every day, and driving an automobile would be more dangerous than fighting a battle.

The Congress of the United States is a group of

persons chosen by the hundred and eighty-five million Americans to make all necessary laws, and to
keep them up to date. It is a big job, and a hard
one, so big and so hard that it never has been and
probably never will be done perfectly. Still for
nearly two hundred years it has been done well
enough to permit the country to grow from a small
and weak one to a large and very powerful one.

Every civilized country has a lawmaking body of
some kind, but no other is exactly like our Congress,
and not many others have lasted as long or worked
as well; so studying Congress is one way to learn a
great deal about the United States.

The Congress of today consists of 535 persons
divided into two groups, one of 100, called the
Senate, the other, of 435, called the House of Representatives. These are the "houses" of Congress,
so-called after the style of the House of Lords and
the House of Commons of the British Parliament.
People generally speak of our houses as the Senate
and the House, but they are sometimes called, like
their British counterparts, the upper and lower
houses.

The great difference in size between the Senate

and the House is because each State has two, and only two Senators, but it has as many Representatives as it has Congressional districts, and the number of its districts depends upon the number of its people. Every State is allowed at least one Representative, and Alaska, Nevada, and Wyoming have only one each. Other more populated States have many more Representatives. For example, New York has forty-one, and California thirty-eight.

The total of 435 members of the House is arbitrary, that is to say, it just happened, without being planned. In the beginning nobody foresaw how big this country would become, and the Constitution makers figured that one Representative for each 30,000 people would be about right. So they decided that each State should have as many districts as its population divided by 30,000. Thus if its population was 180,000, it should have 6 Representatives. If it had 300,000 people, it should have 10, and so on.

The census is taken—that is, the people are counted—every ten years, and by the time of the second census, in 1800, it became plain that with one member to every 30,000 people the House would soon become too large to transact business in an orderly way. If the figure had not been changed, there would today be more than six thousand Representatives, and such a huge mass could never agree on anything.

So the figure was changed after nearly every census. Even so, the House got bigger and bigger until, after the census of 1910, it reached 435. It was decided then to hold the number of Representatives at that point, so now Congress no longer determines the size of a district; instead, the number of people in the whole country is divided by 535, the total of State electoral votes. This is equal to the whole number of members in both the Senate and the House of Representatives. After the census of 1960 the average size of a district worked out at about 336,000, so today each member of the House represents over 11 times as many people as one represented in the first Congress.

A little figuring will show that this is not exact; the representation is *about* 336,000. That figure will not go into the whole population of a State an even number of times except in rare instances. So a member of the House can hardly ever represent exactly 336,000 people. In addition to that, three entire States, Alaska, Nevada, and Wyoming, do not have enough people to constitute an average district, yet, being States, they are entitled to one member of the House. That throws the calculation off again.

Thus while a State always has two Senators, the number of its Representatives varies according to its rank in population. Virginia, once the most populous State with the largest number of Representatives, is now fourteenth, which means that thirteen others have more members of the House.

Despite these limitations on size, each house of Congress is now too large to act as one body except on a few occasions. When it comes to actual voting on a bill, all 100 Senators take part; but before the voting they must decide what is to go into the bill and, equally important, what is to be left out. About this many Senators are likely to have different ideas, which must be argued out.

This cannot be done in the presence of the whole Senate, for two reasons. In the first place, you cannot have a hundred persons in the same room all talking at once, and if you allowed each to talk in turn you might spend weeks, or months, on one bill. In the second place, of the thousands of bills that the Senate must consider at each session, there are many about which only a few Senators know very much. It is good sense, then, when a bill is intro-

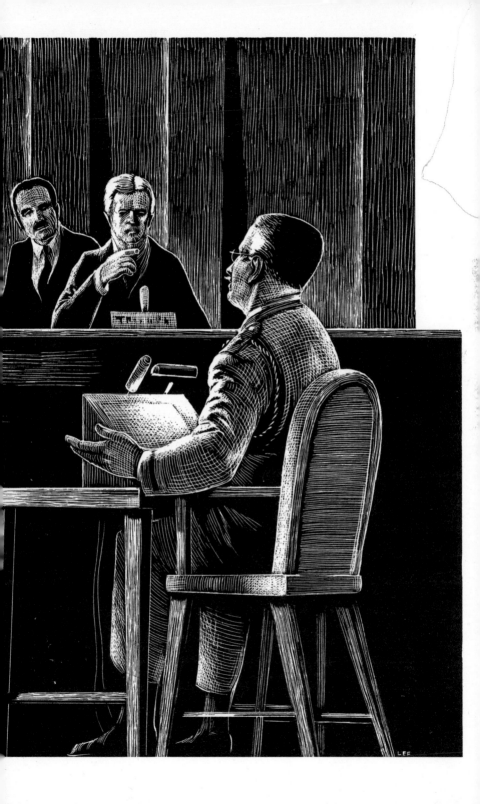

duced to allow those Senators who know most about the subject to examine it first.

That is the system followed. At the first session of each Congress the 100 Senators divide into smaller groups, the Senate committees, and new bills are referred to the committee dealing with that subject. As the House is more than four times as big as the Senate, it is more than four times as necessary for it to work in the same way.

There are three kinds of committees, select, standing, and joint. When anything brand-new comes up, so new that the Senate has seldom, if ever, dealt with it before, a select committee is formed to consider it, and when the matter has been attended to, that committee is discharged and ceases to exist. Occasionally things come up on which both houses must act together, instead of one after the other, and they are referred to joint committees consisting of some Senators and some Representatives. When one house passes a bill and the other house passes a different bill on the same subject, or one house amends a bill passed by the other house, the differences are argued out by a conference committee, which is a kind of select joint committee named for that one job.

A standing committee lasts for the life of the Congress, which is two years. All members belong to at least one standing committee, and when a member is re-elected he is usually appointed to the same standing committee on which he served during his first term. Thus a member who stays in Congress a long time, say ten years, is usually quite expert by the end of that time on the subject with which his committee deals, whether it be agriculture, or banking, or foreign affairs, or what not. Usually he can decide pretty quickly whether or not he likes a new bill.

When a man has served on, say, the Banking and Currency Committee for many years, he has learned, if he has good sense to start with, more about banking and money than some bankers ever know. In the course of its hearings that committee has listened to so many different theories and so many different arguments that seldom does anyone bring up anything that it has not heard before.

Yet the same member who has learned a vast amount about banking may know very little about military affairs; they are handled by another committee. When a banking bill and a military bill are reported, and it is necessary for all members to vote on them, the man who knows banking does not give much study to the military bill. Usually he will choose some member of the Armed Services Committee whose judgment he thinks is good, find out how that man is going to vote on the military bill, and vote the same way.

The members of the Armed Services Committee will do exactly the same thing about the bill relating to banking and currency. In that way Congress gets an amount of work done that otherwise would be impossible. The chances are that most of what it does will be fairly wise.

Many members, when they are first elected, set themselves to master one branch of lawmaking and, as time passes, become expert at it. This is the reason for what is called the "seniority system," under which the member who has been longest on a committee becomes chairman of that committee when his party has a majority in Congress, and the "ranking minority member" when the other party is in power. When there is a change of parties the chairman and the ranking minority member change places.

Unfortunately, some men do not grow wiser as they grow older. They grow crankier. When the seniority system makes one of them chairman of an important committee, there is trouble. In the summer of 1962 an absurd situation arose. The chairmen of two important committees dealing with money bills that had to be worked out jointly fell out over who was to preside at the joint meetings and in which end of the Capitol they should meet. One of these men was eighty-three years old, the other eighty-four, and both were so stubborn that neither would call his committee together and the bills could not be reported. Congress appropriates money for the government on the basis of a year that begins on July 1 and ends on June 30. This is called the fiscal year. Late in June it was suddenly realized that after July 1, when the new fiscal year began, there would be no money to pay many government workers, including Congressmen. Both houses had to pass, in haste, a special law extending last year's appropriation for an extra month—all because the seniority system had made two cranky old men chairmen of important committees.

Most of the members of each standing committee belong to the party that has a majority in its house, but there are always some members of the other party on the committee too. So on disputed bills there are usually two reports, majority and minority. If the majority report is favorable, the minority will be unfavorable, and the other way about. Then it is up to the whole house to decide.

To be a Senator a man or woman must be a citizen of the United States, thirty years old, and living in the State from which he or she is elected. To be a Representative one need be only twenty-five years old, but the other requirements are the same as for the Senators.

Persons born here are citizens by birth. Others may become citizens by going through a process called naturalization, and a naturalized citizen may be elected to Congress like any other, except that he must have been a citizen for seven years before he can become a Representative, and for nine before he can become a Senator.

The Constitution says that any member of Congress must be an inhabitant of the State from which the member is elected. Custom says that a Representative must be an inhabitant, not only of the State, but also of the district to be represented.

The word *inhabitant* is taken to mean *legal resident*. Your legal residence is not the place where you actually are, but the place where you vote.

Members of Congress must live most of the time in Washington, and a member many times re-elected may spend ten, twenty, or thirty years in Washington. But he is considered an inhabitant of the State where he votes, although he may go back to it only on election day and although the house he and his family live in may be in the District of Columbia, or in Maryland, the State surrounding the District.

The term for which a Representative is elected is two years, that of a Senator, six. But the terms of Senators at the start were staggered in such a way that they do not all run out in the same year. About one third of them end every two years, that is to say, every election year. It cannot be exactly one third, because the membership of one hundred cannot be divided exactly by three, so to prevent a vacancy we must elect thirty-four Senators every third election year.

Senators are now elected by vote of all the people of a State, except that when a Senator dies or resigns the Governor of his State may appoint a successor to serve until the next election. The man then chosen serves, not for six years, but only for what remains of the term of the Senator who died or resigned.

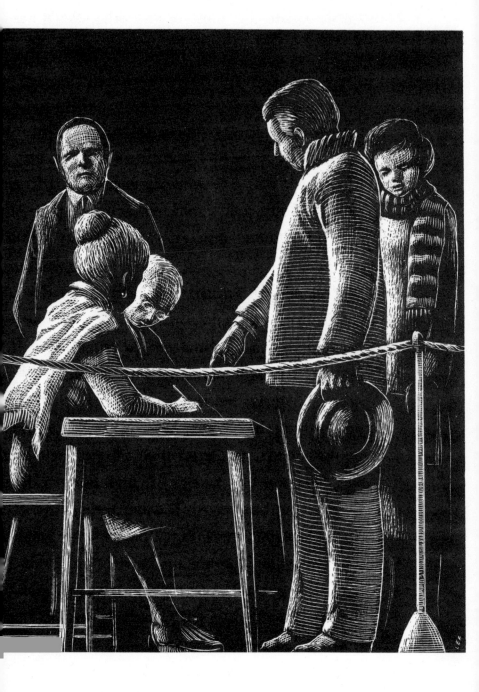

On very rare occasions some State has elected a man whom the Senate deems unfit to sit in that body, usually because most of the other Senators believe that the election was stolen. In that case, the Governor must appoint someone else, for the Constitution says that each house "shall be the judge of the qualifications of its own members." But some State authority must have the right to fill a vacancy, because the Constitution also says that no State, without its consent, "shall be deprived of its equal suffrage in the Senate." Of course, if the Governor refused to appoint another person, the State would be deemed to have consented to have only one Senator.

Representatives also may be elected by the people of the whole State, and when the State is entitled to only one, that is how it is done. But ordinarily the legislature divides the State into a number of districts equal to the number of Representatives to which it is entitled, and the people of each district elect one Representative. Thus a Senator represents his entire State, a Representative only that part of the State that is within his district.

Suppose, then, you were a Representative elected from a medium State—medium in area, medium in population, medium in everything. To avoid hurting anyone's patriotic feelings let us not give it the name of any real State, but call it Old Catawba, the make-believe State about which the novelist Thomas Wolfe wrote.

Old Catawba, let us say, is about fifty thousand square miles in area, has between three and four million people with one city of a quarter of a million, two others of over a hundred thousand, and a dozen between twenty-five and a hundred thousand. This would make it pretty close to an average State.

Your district, then, could be of about average size, that is, with about 336,000 people. The district probably includes some city people and some country people. But it may not be so. By drawing the boundaries of the district in such a way as to weave in and out between the cities, a district could be created with practically all living in it country people.

This is called "gerrymandering." The name comes from the name of a Governor of Massachusetts called Gerry. He once helped create a district so curiously shaped that someone said its map looked like a salamander. But someone else said, "Not salamander, call it gerrymander." Gerrymandering is not often done to make a district include mainly

city, or mainly country people, but it is frequently
done to make it include mainly people of one party
or the other. The State legislature draws the lines,
and if the Republicans are in control they will make
as many Republican districts as they can. The Democrats, when they are in control, will make as many
Democratic districts as they can. The result is that
many members of the House represent very odd-
shaped districts.

Let us suppose, however, that your district is one
that has not been gerrymandered. This means that
you represent both city people and country people,

who, as a rule, are not interested in the same things. You don't want to offend either group, so you have to watch your step. If you give too much attention to what the city people want, the countrymen may grow angry enough to vote against you at the next election. If you neglect the city people, they will act in the same way.

The division between city and country people is only one of many that the members of Congress must watch. Merchants want one kind of thing, manufacturers another, bankers a third. Factory managers and factory workers often desire opposite things. So, sometimes, do Jews and Christians, Catholics and Protestants, rich men and poor men.

With all the good will in the world the Congressman can't please all these people all the time. When demands conflict, he must make up his mind which is better for the whole country, or at least for the whole district, and that isn't always easy. Being a member of Congress isn't a bed of roses, although many people seem to think that it is.

Suppose, though, that an idea comes up that you feel quite sure is for the good of the whole district. You will then be in no doubt as to what you ought to do. You will want to get it enacted into law as soon as possible. In that case, there are three steps that you must take.

The first step is to get the idea written in the form of a bill. If you are wise, you will not often do this yourself, even if you are a lawyer, for writing a bill is somewhat tricky. The language must be so precise that there can be no dispute as to what it means, and it takes practice to be able to write so exactly. The wise member will go to one of a group of lawyers employed by Congress, because they are expert at writing bills. He will put the idea in proper form.

The second step is to introduce the bill, which is done simply by handing it to the clerk of the House or the Senate, who will give it a number and place it on the calendar, that is, the list of bills introduced. It will thereafter be referred to by its number, say, S1234, or HR1234, S meaning Senate and HR House of Representatives. In due time it will be called up and referred to the proper committee.

These two steps are simple enough, but now comes the real work. You must get hold of the chairman, or some important member of the committee —if you are not yourself a member—and arrange for the bill to be considered by the whole committee. Since bills are introduced by the thousands, this is not always easy, but it has to be done, for only in very unusual instances will either House or Senate pay any attention to a bill that has not first been passed upon by a committee. Persuading committee members to consider a bill isn't done by making speeches at them in a public session. It is done by talking to them, man to man, and convincing them that the bill may have merit.

When this is done, the committee may proceed in either of two ways. If the subject is not of great importance, or is one with which the whole committee is familiar, it may be considered in private. The committee merely checks to see that the language is in order and makes any necessary corrections before reporting it. This is done with a great many routine bills.

But if the subject is highly important, or unfamiliar, some members are sure to want more information about it than you can supply. In that case, hearings are held in public, unless the bill concerns something like military affairs that must not be revealed to a possible enemy. To the hearings the committee can summon anyone who is believed to have special information that the committee needs to make up its mind about the bill. Any man summoned to a hearing must go and state on oath that he knows about the subject. If he refuses to go he can be punished for contempt of Congress; if he lies on oath he can be punished for perjury. The only exceptions are the President of the United States and a Justice of the Supreme Court. They cannot be compelled to appear at a hearing, because they belong to different, but equal, branches of the government and the legislative cannot give orders to either the executive or the judiciary. A man working for one of these branches—the President's secretary, for example—can be summoned, but if the President forbids him to go he cannot be punished for refusing, for that would be equal to punishing the President.

Generally speaking, though, men who favor a bill are glad to appear at a hearing and tell what they know in its favor. Those who oppose it are frequently even more anxious to appear and tell what they think is wrong with it. Since all these people are usually well-informed, what is said at committee hearings is often more important and more interesting than what is said on the floor of either house. That is why the people who sit in the public galleries and listen to the speeches don't see or hear much of the real work of Congress.

When you have persuaded the committee, especially if it is a standing committee, to report your bill favorably, that is, recommend that the bill be passed, your battle is more than half-won. Other members are inclined to take the advice of the committee, because they know more about the subject than members who have not attended the hearings and have not been accustomed to dealing with bills on the same subject. If a favorable report is unanimous, it is ten to one that the bill will pass, since there is then no reason for either Democrats or Republicans to vote against it.

Even on a disputed matter, it is fair to say that a bill favorably reported is already half passed. That is because the committee members voting favorably usually belong to the majority party if they have enough votes to win. The majority in either Senate or House belongs to their party and will ordinarily vote as they did in the committee.

If, however, the committee decides it dislikes your idea, it may report your bill unfavorably. More often it quietly forgets the whole business, and your bill, as people say, "dies in committee."

When the whole House votes in favor of your bill, it goes from the House to the Senate, and the process

is repeated. If the second vote is also favorable, the bill is sent to the President. If he approves it, he signs it, and the instant he signs it your bill becomes law.

But the President does not have to sign your bill. He can send it back to the House, or the Senate if it originated there, with a message explaining his objections. This is called a veto. Another vote is then taken, and if two thirds of the members still vote favorably, the vetoed bill goes to the other house. If two thirds of its members also vote favorably, the bill becomes a law without the President's signature. That is called "overriding the veto," and it takes two thirds of both houses to do it.

There is one exception to this. If the President neither signs the bill nor sends it back within ten days, the bill becomes law unless Congress has adjourned before the ten days are up, in which case it does not become law. The object of this is to prevent Congress' playing a trick on the President by passing bills it knows he dislikes and then adjourning before he has time to veto them.

But this rule leaves the way open for a trick by the President. Sometimes a Congress that doesn't like the President will pass, near the end of the session, a bill that some people will blame him for signing and others will blame him for vetoing. If he knows that Congress is going to adjourn within four or five days, he will probably do nothing. Instead of either signing or vetoing the bill, he will, as the saying is, put the bill in his pocket, and when Congress adjourns it is dead. This is called a "pocket veto."

There are some minor differences in the ways that the Senate and the House go about their work, but in general they follow the same plan. Differences are that the House has twenty standing committees, the Senate only sixteen, and some committees differ in name, as the House Committee on Foreign Affairs and the Senate Committee on Foreign Relations.

But if you were a Representative from Old Catawba, you would find that a great deal of your work has nothing to do with getting bills passed. You would spend most of your time on things about which there is not one word in the Constitution.

This is not anybody's fault. It is due to the simple fact that the world today is very different from what it was in 1787, and nobody at that time could imagine what it was going to be like today. The marvel of the Constitution is that it still works pretty well in a world that the men of 1787 could not imagine.

As a result, the member from Old Catawba does a great deal that Washington and Franklin and Madison never dreamed he would be asked to do. This is true especially of the Representatives. A Senator represents a whole State, a Representative only one district; neither can possibly know by sight and name all the people he represents. A Representative, however, can come closer to it than a Senator, so the people of his district feel that he is closer to them than the Senator. Therefore, when they want anything at Washington, it is usually to their Representative that they apply first.

Now there are millions of Americans who live to be old men and women and die without ever feeling the need to ask anything of their Representative, and there are many others who come into direct contact with the government at Washington only once in a lifetime. But everybody, unless he either makes no money or has a vast number of children, pays income tax, and there is hardly any man in business who does not have some kind of dealings with the government. When any difficulty comes up in this connection, he thinks immediately of his Representative and asks for his help.

Most of the time the member of Congress is glad to give it, for in that way he makes friends who will vote for him at the next election. But helping his constituents takes time. Even if it is as small a matter as getting a ticket of admission to the visitors' gallery, it takes a minute or two, and often it is something more complicated. Many of the people who call on the member do so because they think the government has somehow done them wrong. It may be a businessman who thinks he is being required to pay more taxes than he is justly due to pay, or it may be a woman who thinks her son is being mistreated in the army, or it may be someone who complains that the postmaster in his town is no good, or it may be any one of a thousand other things.

The least of these requests for help usually means that the Representative must make a phone call or write a letter. If the person complaining is not a mere crank, but has a real grievance, it may take many phone calls, letters, and personal interviews to straighten out the matter. It is no wonder that the member of Congress needs much office room and many assistants to enable him to keep up with his work.

This, remember, is not the job laid out for him in the Constitution. All these things he must do to keep the good will of the people who voted for him and gave him a chance to work at his Constitutional job, which is lawmaking.

In general, the making of laws is equally the business of both houses, but there are two exceptions. "All bills for raising revenue," says the Constitution, "shall originate in the House of Representatives," although the Senate must consent before they become law. The Senate may also amend a revenue bill if the House consents. The reason for this was that until 1913 Senators were not elected directly by the people, but by the members of the State legislatures, and so were considered one step removed from the people. Raising revenue usually means levying taxes, and being taxed is a subject on which the people are quite sensitive. Thus it was thought best to have the House, whose members are closer to the people, be the first to propose any new tax.

The other exception limits the President's power to make treaties and appoint officers of the government, other than minor ones. In both cases the President must act "by and with the advice and consent of the Senate." Since President Washington's day, this has usually meant "consent," for it has not been practical for the Senate to do much advising on such matters. The reason for this was never publicly stated by the makers of the Constitution, but probably it was their belief that Senators, chosen by the legislatures, would be wiser and better men than Representatives, chosen by the people.

There is another difference between House and Senate that often confuses people, although it is simple enough if one knows how it happened. The House of Representatives chooses its own presiding officer. The Senate does not. The Constitution says that the Vice-President of the United States shall be president of the Senate, but shall have no vote except in case of a tie.

There are two reasons for this. One is that the Constitution provides nothing else for the Vice-President to do, except hang around waiting for something to happen to the President.

The other is more important. There is little doubt that the writers of the Constitution thought of the Senate as an upper house, something like the House of Lords. Therefore, its chief officer would be the highest in the legislative branch of the government. Yet they were determined that all States should be equally represented in the Senate. Then to permit one State to have a Senator who outranked all other Senators would give that State an edge, however slight. Here, then, was something for the Vice-President to do, and also an answer to a problem.

But the Vice-President belongs to the executive branch, the Senate to the legislative. To have a man from one branch be the highest officer of another branch wouldn't do. That problem was solved by recognizing the presiding officer of the House as the highest legislative officer, ranking with the President and the Chief Justice.

The House elects one of its own members as Speaker and, as a member, he may vote on any bill, although he usually does not, except in case of a tie, or when some bill comes up on which he is anxious to have it on record that he voted for or against it. When a bill is under discussion, he has the right to call some other member to the chair to preside while he goes down and makes a speech from the floor. But this happens rarely, and never except on some matter of great importance.

The Senators do, however, elect one of their own

number to preside when the Vice-President is absent. His title is President *pro tempore,* meaning "for the time being," and it is considered a high honor, but not a powerful office, such as the Speakership.

In both House and Senate the members of each party select one of their number to act as leader. They are highly important men, but they are party officials, not officers of Congress. The business of each is to try to hold his party together on all important measures. This is a matter of politics, the art of winning elections, not statecraft, the art of governing the country. The majority leader frequently, and the minority leader sometimes, must support a measure simply because his party has agreed upon it, although in his own opinion it is unwise. But that is due to the way the parties are organized, not to the way the Constitution was written.

Many of the methods of Congress have odd beginnings. For instance, that curious operation called the filibuster is a historical survival of the old idea that every member of Congress should enjoy absolute freedom of speech. This was the rule in the first Congress, but the House soon grew so large that if every member were allowed to do all the talking he liked, nothing would ever get done. So the House soon adopted rules limiting the time that one member can hold the floor, and the rules have grown stricter as the House has grown larger.

But the Senate, being smaller, has clung to the old idea. Senators have also discovered that unlimited debate is a fine way to stop action. As long as one Senator is making a speech, nothing else can be done. When a Senator, or, more often, a small group of Senators, realizes that an objectionable bill is going to pass if it comes to a vote, they kill time by talking endlessly, thereby preventing a vote. If the end of the session is near, and much urgent business remains to be done, the majority will sometimes submit and abandon the bill, even though they approve it.

The word *filibuster* originally meant a man who goes into a country with which his own is at peace and there starts a war. So a Senator who conducts a war of his own against the majority is given the name of filibuster, and his operation is called filibustering.

This, then, is a general picture of how Congress does its work today.

The Beginnings of Congress

CONGRESS, AS WE KNOW IT, was established in 1789, when the Constitution of the United States, having been ratified by nine of the original thirteen States, became the supreme law of the land. The word, indeed, had been used long before that. The first name of this country was, "The United States of America in Congress Assembled," from which you might guess — and you would be right — that the Congress was the whole government.

The common noun congress, spelled with a small c, means a getting together, and when the thirteen British colonies in North America got together to throw off the rule of the British king they called their meeting by that name. Of course, three million people couldn't get together in one room, so each colony sent a few representatives, and the first formal agreement among those representatives was

called the Articles of Confederation. It is in the Articles that you will find the name, "The United States of America in Congress Assembled."

But the Articles were so loose and vague that it was impossible to set up a good government under them, and four years after the end of the Revolutionary War the Congress called a special convention to work out something better. This was the famous Constitutional Convention that met in Philadelphia and wrote our present Constitution.

One trouble with the Articles was that the Congress, in trying to be everything, had ended by being not much of anything, so the members of the Convention decided to correct that. What they did was split the powers of government three ways. The legislative, the lawmaking power, they left with Congress. The executive, the power to enforce the law after it is made, they gave to the President. The judicial, the power to decide exactly what the law means, they gave to the Supreme Court.

In theory this took away two thirds of the power of Congress, but in fact it didn't work out that way. Under the new system Congress retained only the legislative power, but that alone, in a strong government, made it many times as powerful as it had been when it was trying to be everything in a weak government.

The States had all stood together against the British, and they called themselves united. In fact, they were a long way from united, they did not even like each other much, and as soon as the British army left their differences became very plain. All sorts of quarrels broke out, and more than once they came close to actual fighting. For four years things went steadily from bad to worse.

When the Constitutional Convention met at Philadelphia in 1787 the members found that when the quarreling among the States was over something that could be seen and touched—a piece of land, say, or a navigation channel, or a bridge, or a road— matters could usually be arranged rather quickly. But when it was over something that could be neither seen nor touched, especially something that did not then exist, but might come later, the quarrel was very troublesome indeed.

Rhode Island, for instance, the smallest of the States, was free and independent in 1787, but Rhode Island adjoined Connecticut, which was bigger, and Massachusetts, which was very much bigger. Neither State, at the time, was trying to oppress Rhode

Island, but what about the future? Would not the day come when the big States would decide to blot out the little ones, taking over their territory and people?

On the other hand, in the Confederation Rhode Island and Delaware, smallest of the States, could outvote Virginia, several times larger than both of them, since each State had one vote. They could also cancel the votes of Virginia and Pennsylvania, the two largest States. Where was the fairness in that?

The dispute over how the States should be represented in the legislature very nearly wrecked the Convention and did keep it in session through a long, hot summer. Its final solution fixed the make-up of Congress, for the solution was that every State should have an equal number of votes (two) in the Senate, regardless of its size, and a number of votes in the House according to its size.

Since every bill must pass both houses before it becomes law, the Senate prevents the large States from oppressing the small ones, and the House makes it impossible for the small States to dictate to the large ones. What nobody foresaw was the creation of States with very large areas and very few people, but now we have three with fewer people than there are supposed to be in a single Congressional district. Some writers make fun of this fact. They say that Senators from those States represent more coyotes and jack rabbits than people which, they say, is not right. But such arguments are a waste of time, because a State, once admitted to the Union, cannot be abolished except by its own consent.

Thus the scheme worked out in 1787 was not quite perfect, but it has worked pretty well for nearly two hundred years. For that reason Americans are willing to listen to anyone who has an idea for improving the system, but they pay little attention to those wild men who want to knock down the whole thing and build a new government from the ground up.

It was decided that the headquarters of the Federal government should be built on land given by the State of Maryland (Virginia gave some, too, but she got her part back in 1846). George Washington and a city planner chosen by him, Pierre Charles L'Enfant, a Frenchman who had joined the American army during the Revolution and had come to be a major of engineers, looked over the ground to lay out the streets and decide where the chief public buildings should go.

For the President's house they chose a spot near the village of Georgetown, which was on the bank of the Potomac River. For the houses of Congress —incidentally, for the Supreme Court, too, but it was Congress that they thought of chiefly—they went back a mile from the President's house, and located the building on the top of a bluff eighty-eight feet high, from which one could look down to and across the river to the Virginia hills on the other side. It is a magnificent site, by far the finest in the city.

Here, in 1793, they began building what is now the part of the Capitol between the central section and the Senate wing, and into this part Congress moved in 1800 and the Supreme Court in 1801. In 1807 they began to build the corresponding part on the other side, and in 1811 the House of Representatives moved into it, leaving a gap where the central section is now. In 1814 the British army burned both sections, as well as the President's house. The sandstone walls were left standing, but blackened with smoke and soot, so when the buildings were repaired the walls were painted white. Then came the central section, with a low dome, and finally two great wings, on the north for the Senate, on the South for the House, with the present high dome in the center.

Thus the Capitol was not built all at once according to a single plan, but was put together by bits and pieces. The latest thing done to it was finished in 1961, when the eastern face of the central section was pushed out thirty-two feet to bring it into line with the two wings. Yet in spite of having been pieced together over a period of a hundred and sixty-eight years, it has the appearance of a single building, stately and dignified. In that, it is like the country—by no means what it started out to be, but unmistakably one, and very great.

At the time of the Revolution all educated Americans, like educated men everywhere, knew Latin. The better-educated knew Greek, too, but they all knew Latin, and in learning that language had learned a great deal about ancient Rome. So when Americans started to set up a republic, they naturally studied the Roman republic, the most famous republic of the ancient world, and found in it a great deal to admire. They gave to one house of Congress the Roman name of Senate, and for the

other, instead of the British name Commons, they chose Representatives, from the Latin *representare.* It is not surprising, then, that to the building where Congress was to meet they gave the name of the building where the Roman Senate met, and called it the Capitol.

Men constantly apply old names to new things. The presiding officer of the House of Representatives is called the Speaker, because in England, long before this country existed, whenever the Commons had anything to say to the king they let their leader do the talking, and the rest remained respectfully silent while he spoke for the House. We have no king to speak to, and our President speaks to Congress, instead of the other way about. But the chief officer of the house that corresponds to the English House of Commons is still the Speaker.

One change in our system is not yet quite complete. It is in the way we refer to the legislative body. In the old days, it was always "the Congress." Now it is usually "Congress," except when we mean the body that was sitting at a particular time. For instance, the one sitting when this book was written was "the eighty-seventh Congress."

This comes from the fact that men are chosen to

be members of the House of Representatives for two years, and of the Senate for six. This requires us to vote, every second year, for a completely new House and for one third of the Senate. The life of *a* Congress is from election to election, that is to say, two years; yet Congress has existed ever since the Constitution was adopted. "Congress," therefore, means the whole succession of Congresses, eighty-seven in number up to 1963, and "the Congress" is the one sitting at a specific date, as "the Congress that impeached President Johnson," or "the Congress at the time of the battle of Pearl Harbor." But this distinction is not, or at least it is not yet, a hard-and-fast rule.

An American Congress may have adjourned its sessions and its members may have scattered to their homes, but they are still members to the day their terms expire, and the President may call them into extra session at any time. At noon on January 3, 1963, the eighty-seventh Congress ceased to exist, but at the same instant the eighty-eighth Congress came into existence. Its members could not act until they had taken the oath of office, but they were members from the stroke of noon. Two thirds of the Senate, of course, had already been sworn in. Since we can never be without *a* Congress, it is accurate to say that Congress, as a branch of government, is perpetual.

But while its existence as a branch of the government has never changed, the way it acts and the power it exerts have varied often and in many respects. Starting out pretty much as an imitation of the British Parliament, little by little it has dropped British ways of acting and adopted new ways of its own, but always in the knowledge that whatever it does must be within the law as it is found in the Constitution. Thus in spite of all its new schemes and new duties, it remains the same branch of government that was set up in 1789. A Frenchman once said of the city of Paris, "The more it changes, the more it is the same thing," and his words might apply to Congress.

The power of Congress has also sometimes gone up and sometimes gone down, according to circumstances. One of those circumstances, and an important one, is the character of the man who happens to be President, and of the nine who are Justices of the Supreme Court. They can influence Congress very strongly, if they are strong, and can be influenced by Congress, if they are weak. The struggle for power among them is the larger part of the history of politics in the United States.

One measure of the way Congress has changed is presented by two figures. In the first Congress, which met under President Washington, 258 bills were introduced. In the eighty-fifth, the third one under President Eisenhower, 17,230 were introduced. In the first Congress, of the 258 bills introduced, 94 passed, which is a little more than 36 per cent. In the eighty-fifth, of the 17,230 bills introduced, 1292 passed, barely more than 7 per cent.

In the old days, therefore, getting a bill introduced in Congress meant a great deal more than it means now. With a 7 per cent, as against a 36 per cent chance of passage, one may say that it meant five times as much.

The impressive figure, though, is the number of bills—more than 17,000 in one Congress. It would appear, at first, that Congress is playing a much more important part in running the country than it played in those early days. This is the fact, but it must not be forgotten that today there is a great deal more of a country to run. Innumerable new kinds of work and play and means of getting about have appeared, and almost every one of them calls for some kind of regulation and direction by some kind of government, often the Federal government.

There is no doubt whatever that the ordinary American has to deal with the United States government much more often than he had to when Washington, or John Adams, was President. Take, for example, heating the house in winter. Even when Abraham Lincoln was President the great majority of Americans were farmers and lived in the country. For heat the farmer cut down a tree or two in his own wood lot. He sawed it into convenient lengths himself, split it himself, hauled it and stacked it himself. Today most Americans live in cities, where they burn coal, or oil, or gas for heat. These things are usually brought from far away by a series of companies — a coal-mining or oil-producing company, a railroad or pipeline company, and a retail fuel company whose trucks come to the man's house. If he burns oil or gas he will never touch it himself, and never see most of the men who do handle it.

Against such big companies one man would be helpless if there were no laws to protect him. We must have laws touching all these matters, and if the product passes from one State into another,

Congress must make the laws because the Constitution says that Congress, nobody else, shall regulate interstate commerce. Thus when people complain, as some are always complaining, that Congress is taking away our liberties, they are usually—not always, but usually—wrong. What is restricting our liberty is not Congress, but the way we live. When nearly two hundred million people live on the same ground that three million lived on in 1776, the two hundred million simply can't move about as freely as the three million did. There isn't room enough, and many rules must be made to prevent their running into each other.

Some people believe that the men who made the Constitution expected, or at least hoped, to set up a system in which all three branches of the government would work together happily and smoothly, each loyally supporting the other two. They had no such idea, as anyone can easily discover by reading *The Federalist*, the book of essays in which Madison, Hamilton, and Jay, all of whom were there, explained what the members of the Convention actually had in mind.

The Founding Fathers believed in the maxim, "All power tends to extend itself." They knew, before Lord Acton put it into words, that "All power tends to corrupt and absolute power corrupts absolutely." Therefore, they were determined that no man, and no one branch of government, should ever have absolute power in the United States.

The way to prevent one power from extending itself too far is, of course, to set up another power that will stop it. And that is what the Constitution does. We call it "the system of checks and balances." What it means is that if the President begins to get too strong, Congress and the Supreme Court will stop him; if Congress gets too strong, the President and the Supreme Court will stop it; and if the Supreme Court threatens to take over all power, the President and Congress will stop it.

This doesn't make for peace and quiet in the government. On the contrary, it means fighting pretty much all the time. Good people, reading the history of the United States and learning how often the President and Congress, or the President and the Court, or the Court and Congress were fighting, are shocked, and think it shows that there must be a terrible fault in our system. But the writers of the Constitution wouldn't have been shocked. They would have thought it a good thing, for as long as the three branches check and balance each other, none will get so strong that it can take freedom from the people.

One may agree generally with this system, and yet see how there might be times when the checks and balances, if they were exactly equal, might stop all three branches from doing something that very much needs to be done. But we have found by experience that they never are exactly equal. What happens is that power sways back and forth, from one branch to another.

There have been times when Congress seemed about to take over everything. There have been other times—usually in war—when the President was so much like a dictator that one could hardly see the difference. There have been times when the Supreme Court seemed determined to prevent Congress and the President from doing what both thought was good for the country. But such times have always been short. They were usually connected with some great crisis that had the country tremendously excited, and when the crisis passed the balance of power swung back.

Check and Balance

URING THE EIGHT YEARS when Washington was President, and the four when John Adams followed him, the country was still small and Congress was not called on to do a great deal. A man could be a member and still have time to practice law, or run a farm, or manage a store. Nobody, in Congress or in the other branches, was certain how this new kind of government was going to work out, so everyone was inclined to move carefully, feeling his way along rather than plunging ahead. Disagreement was the exception, rather than the rule.

But Washington's first term was not over when opinion began to divide, and his second term had hardly started when the split became very clear. Gradually everybody took sides on this question: should the central government build up its power as fast as it could, or should it leave power in the hands of the States as long as it could?

That was the beginning of political parties in this country. The people who felt that the central government should become as powerful as possible as soon as possible followed Alexander Hamilton as their leader. Those who thought the central government should not try to take additional power until it had to followed Thomas Jefferson.

A point that students are likely to overlook, although it is most important, is that neither theory was absolute. Hamilton never claimed that the Federal government should have all power. Jefferson never claimed that it should always remain no stronger than it was when he became President. Nobody was in favor of going backward, or even of standing still; the quarrel was over how fast to move forward.

The United States is almost unique among the nations in that it has never had a major party that was against the whole system. Seeing this, many foreigners have decided that there is no real difference between Republicans and Democrats, and that we have only one genuine party. On our part, it is hard for us to imagine how it feels to know that the loss of an election will mean the loss of the whole system of government.

After 1789, when the French rose against their king as we had risen against George III, another difference developed between Hamilton and Jefferson. It was in the way they looked at the French Revolution. Hamilton was shocked and alarmed, Jefferson pleased. However, when the French, not content with deposing the king, proceeded to cut off his head, and the queen's, and those of a great many people whose only crime was being noblemen, the thing got to be too much even for Jefferson. As Secretary of State, he recommended throwing out the French minister, Genêt, which President Washington did.

When John Adams became the second President in 1797, events were moving the United States straight toward war with France. This suited Hamilton perfectly, because he had always wanted to make England our firmest friend and he thought war with France would do it. Besides, he had always wanted to command an army and had managed to get a commission as a reserve major general. In the Revolution he had been only a colonel, and a staff officer at that.

But war didn't suit John Adams, and that led to

the first big fight between a President and Congress. Hamilton was not himself a member, but everyone knew that he, not the President, was the real leader of the Federal Party in Congress. So when Adams seized the first opportunity to smooth things over with France, Hamilton and his friends in Congress were furious, and tore into the President, even though he was of their own party.

This was quite all right with Jefferson, whom Adams had beaten for the Presidency by seventy-one to sixty-eight electoral votes. If the Federalists wanted to destroy their own party, he was happy to encourage them. And that is just what they did. From that time on they never won another Presidential election, and in 1814 they were finished when some of their more foolish leaders—Hamilton had then been dead ten years—tried to persuade New England to leave the Union.

At the time Adams and Congress were quarreling over France, nobody understood just what was happening. Everybody was furious and ready to blame everybody else. The President was sure that Hamilton had betrayed him. Hamilton suspected that Jefferson had somehow pulled a slick trick, although he couldn't say exactly how. Jefferson said publicly that the whole Federalist crew were bent on pulling down the republic and bringing back a king.

No doubt this was natural. Angry men seldom see things as they really are, and are inclined to blame some enemy for the results of their own mistakes. What actually happened was that the system of checks and balances worked. The Constitution says that all dealings with foreign nations shall be handled by the President, except that only Congress may declare war, and when the President makes a permanent treaty two thirds of the Senate must consent. So when the Federalist members tried to tell Adams how to deal with France, Congress was trying to grab some of the President's power, and the President checked it.

Hamilton had played a large part in making the Constitution, and both Adams and Jefferson, although they were in Europe at the time of the Convention, had studied it with the greatest care. Yet when the thing worked exactly as it was intended and expected to work, they were all astonished and inclined to suspect that some kind of devilment was going on. It simply shows that men, even great men, when their plans are suddenly upset can lose their tempers and their judgment.

The next great collision was between Congress and the Supreme Court. One of the first things Congress did in 1789 was to pass a Judiciary Act saying that the Chief Justice should have four Associate Justices on the Supreme Court, along with a great many other rules saying how judges and lawyers must act in trying cases, and so on. A second act, saying that the courts might issue a writ, called a *mandamus*, commanding an officer of the government to do his Constitutional duty, in case he refused, was passed during the administration of John Adams.

The question of using such a writ first came up in the famous case of *Marbury versus Madison*, and its decision abolished forever the idea that the American Congress was a sort of copy of the British Parliament. For the Court decided—and all the world believes that the deciding was really done by John Marshall, Chief Justice and by far the strongest of the five men on the Court—that Congress, in passing a bill allowing the Court to issue such writs against the executive, had in effect amended the

Constitution, which Congress cannot do. An act of Congress that violates the Constitution is no law, and the courts are not bound by it.

All the rest of that decision matters little, and in fact most of the rest has since been reversed by the Court itself; but the point that the Supreme Court may, in certain circumstances, declare that an act of Congress is no law established the great difference between the Congress of the United States and the Parliament of Great Britain. Under no circumstances may any authority declare that an act of Parliament is no law, and Congress had believed that it had equal power in this country.

But the system of checks and balances had worked again, the Supreme Court doing the checking this time. Looking back on it, it seems to have been a high-handed piece of business, for in claiming the right to nullify an act of Congress, Marshall himself was extending the power of the Court enormously, that is, he was doing what he said Congress could not do.

Most people decided, though, that maybe it wasn't a bad thing to have some authority that could restrain Congress from straying beyond the bounds of the Constitution. Thus there came to be less and less opposition to the rule in *Marbury versus Madison,* and it has stood ever since.

President Adams, representing the executive branch, had checked Congress, the legislative. Then Chief Justice Marshall, representing the judiciary, had checked it. But it was not always so. Now and then the legislative branch, Congress, has done some checking of the others.

The first startling instance occurred in 1832 and 1833, when the Union was threatened with destruction while Andrew Jackson was President. The "reign of Andrew the First," as some people choose to call the administration of President Jackson, was certainly the noisiest up to that time in American history. It was one big battle after another, but the one that affected the position of Congress the most was the fight that followed when the State of South Carolina announced that she would not obey a tariff law passed by Congress. The South Carolinians declared that the law was unjust to them, and today many historians agree that it was. The proper remedy, of course, was to get the law changed, but the South Carolinians thought they had not much chance of doing that, so the State legislature simply proclaimed that, whatever it might be elsewhere, in South Carolina the law was "null," that is to say, nothing. That is why the movement is called Nullification.

To Andrew Jackson, President of the United States, that was not only rebellion against the nation, it was also a personal insult to him. If Nullification had been allowed to succeed, Jackson might have been left President of the rest of the country, but not of South Carolina, and he was not the man to let anybody make him a part President. He did not like the South Carolina leader, John C. Calhoun, anyhow, and he suspected Calhoun of having stirred up the quarrel to make trouble for him. Naturally, he was in a towering rage.

As a matter of fact, it was the tariff law, not Calhoun, that started the row, but there is no doubt whatever that Calhoun helped it along. He had a low opinion of Jackson, whom he regarded as nothing but a Tennessee hillbilly, who ought never to have become President. Neither man was disposed to yield one inch to the other. In South Carolina they called out the militia—the state troops corresponding to the National Guard of today—and Jackson began ordering the regular army and the navy to move into position to invade South Carolina.

There was great excitement, and everybody was watching those two men so closely that they did not pay much attention to anything else. Even to this day, when Nullification is mentioned, many people think of it as mainly, if not altogether, a fight between Jackson and Calhoun.

So it was, but there was a third person involved who didn't like either of the other two, and who very much disliked seeing their fight split the country. He was Henry Clay, next to Jackson the smartest politician in the country and a much smoother operator. Clay had had a hand in making the tariff to which South Carolina objected, for his State, Kentucky, grew much hemp, used in making rope, and Clay got a heavy duty laid on foreign hemp and rope. He was not so devoted to the hemp growers, however, that he would risk civil war for their benefit. He was a Senator, and before that had been Speaker of the House, so he knew Congress as well as any man in it, and far better than most.

Clay went to work to prevent a war, and he had to work fast and furiously. He knew he couldn't do anything with South Carolina, so his only chance was to prevent the President from going too far, and stopping Andrew Jackson from doing anything that

he thought he ought to do was no easy task. Clay knew better than to defy the President. That would have set off an explosion instantly. The way to stop him was to take away his excuse for acting, and that is what Clay did. By fast talking, not so much in speeches on the floor as by arguing with members one at a time, he convinced a majority that the tariff law was a bad one, and he persuaded both houses to pass a new act repealing the old one, not all at once, but in a series of steps. That gave South Carolina a chance to drop Nullification, which, in turn, left Jackson no reason to order the army into the State. At heart both Jackson and Calhoun were glad to get out of the mess, Calhoun because no other State had backed up South Carolina, Jackson because he was none too sure that he had troops and ships enough to do the job.

This was an instance in which Congress checked the President. The thing was done so smoothly that people frequently overlook that it was done at all. But it was. The system of checks and balances came into play to hold back a furious President. Andrew Jackson knew that it was the best thing that could have happened, but at that he half regretted that the fight didn't go on to a finish. Many years later he told a friend that he was sorry to have missed a chance to hang John C. Calhoun.

Another thing that this affair did was to begin to show everyone, including Congress, how carefully Congress must consider all the effects of its work. When that tariff bill came to a vote, it is probable that four fifths of the members were thinking only of its effect on something back home, as Clay was certainly thinking of its effect on the market for Kentucky hemp. To some it might have made no difference if they had known that they were actually voting to split the country; they would have gone ahead and voted for their selfish interest anyhow. But a majority would not have done so. Clay proved that when he put over his compromise. Congress cannot always think of politics. That is not fully realized even yet, but it began to be realized when that tariff bill nearly started a war.

When a first-rate man appears in any group, he throws into the shade a dozen ordinary men, and when people think of the group they think of him. For about thirty years after 1820 Congress had not one, but three, who were more than first-rate, who were really great statesmen. They were Henry Clay, of Kentucky, John C. Calhoun, of South Carolina, and Daniel Webster, of Massachusetts. When people think of Congress in this period they always think of these three. A New Englander will name them as Webster, Clay, and Calhoun, a Southerner as Calhoun, Clay, and Webster, a Westerner as Clay, Webster, and Calhoun, but all sections tend to think of the three as about all there was to Congress in those days.

Of course, it isn't true. In both the House and the Senate at that time there were many other men almost as able as these. Yet it is a fact that if you wish to know how Congress developed, the quickest and easiest way is to study what these three were doing.

Cynics will say that the main thing that each of them was doing was trying to make himself President. In a sense it is true, but the significant thing was the way in which they went about it. These were years in which great changes were following each other with great speed. The railroad and the telegraph were new inventions that helped the factories to increase greatly. This, in turn, caused the rapid growth of cities, and the cities were making the country quite different from what it had been before.

But we were slow to understand that our political system had to change too, in order to fit the new ways of living and doing business. It was Congress, especially such men as Clay, Calhoun, and Webster, that had the job of designing the changes in the political system and persuading the people to accept them. It was a hard job, a terrific job. In the end, it proved too hard for Congress, and that is why we crashed into the Civil War, the most terrible war that we ever fought.

The biggest of all the necessary changes, the one on which most of the others depended, was that of finding some better labor system than Negro slavery. Slavery was bad, but starvation was worse, and even Southerners as great as Washington and Jefferson honestly couldn't see how slavery could be abolished without starving all the Negroes and most of the whites in the South. They were not far wrong. When at last slavery was abolished by the Civil War, many years followed in which much of the South was on the very verge of famine.

Clay, Calhoun, and Webster knew, as wise men have always known, that when men dispute over some subject about which nobody knows the whole truth, it is easy for them to proceed from disputing to savage fighting. In 1820, when slavery first came to be seriously debated in Congress, Jefferson, by that time an old man long since retired from public office, was as alarmed as if he had heard "a fire bell in the night," and many men shared his uneasiness. Certainly Clay, Calhoun, and Webster shared it, and for thirty years it was their main purpose to keep the debate from breaking into war.

We often think of them in a different way. Calhoun defended the Southern interest, Webster the Northern, and it is sometimes said that these two urged the country toward war, with only Clay, in between, trying to prevent it. But the truth is that all three tried to prevent it, and did prevent it, time after time. Looking back, we can see how their best efforts sometimes seemed to make war more certain, but that was not their purpose. Their last great effort was in 1850, when the three combined to push through Congress the group of laws known as the Compromise of 1850, which staved off the war for another ten years. By the end of 1852 all three had died.

After the disappearance of the men who worked out the great Compromise, the argument over slavery grew more and more bitter, swallowing up arguments over all other questions. The dispute was leading straight toward war, as everyone could see. Now slavery was only to a minor extent a legal question. A legal question is answered by finding out what the law actually is; but the question with regard to slavery was what the law should be. That is to say, it was mainly a question of policy, a political question. Political questions can be answered only by the lawmakers, who decide what the law shall be.

Unfortunately, the Chief Justice at the time, Roger B. Taney, although he was an able and learned man, forgot this, or would not believe it. The Court had before it the case of a Negro named Dred Scott, and the Chief Justice, who wrote the opinion, undertook to decide not only the case of Dred Scott, but the whole slavery issue. Right there he was trying to take over the power of Congress, which alone can decide political questions. Taney said that not only was Dred Scott a slave, but that he couldn't be made free by any act of Congress, because Congress had no right to interfere with slavery in any way.

Millions of Americans felt that this simply wasn't so. They flatly refused to admit that the Court, by saying that a thing is true, can make it true when it

isn't. What the Dred Scott decision actually did was not to settle the slavery question, but to reduce confidence in the Supreme Court. Even in the South the wiser kind of men knew that Taney had gone too far and had tried to seize power that did not belong to the judiciary.

Taney's friends say—and they may be right—that his only thought was to prevent war. But all he did was hasten its coming. If slavery couldn't be handled by law, it would be handled by violence, and it was. The Civil War reversed the Dred Scott decision, but at terrible cost. Yet it could have been foreseen and, in fact, it was foreseen. The makers of the Constitution knew that when checks and balances fail, men will resort to blood and iron, which is what they did in 1861.

The war smashed slavery, but the clincher was put on after the war when the people adopted the three antislavery amendments (the thirteenth, fourteenth, and fifteenth). After all, in any such case the last word is with the people. It was they who decreed that Congress did have power to interfere with slavery, and now it is generally agreed that it has power to deal with anything else that seems to offer a threat to the nation.

While the Court was still in bad favor, because it had tried to seize power that did not belong to it, another clash came, this time between the legislative and the executive. The Constitution says that Congress, and only Congress, shall have the right to declare war. But it also says that in time of war, as at all other times, the President shall be the commander in chief of all the armed forces; and it is certain that no commander can command successfully if someone is always interfering with his orders.

Soon after the beginning of the fighting in the Civil War, Congress set up a Select Committee on the Conduct of the War, and it created so much trouble that if anybody but Abraham Lincoln had been President it would almost certainly have lost the war. The situation was bad enough, without any meddling by Congress. The United States army was small, had few trained officers, and of those few some of the best as, for instance, Lee, Longstreet, Beauregard, and the two Johnstons, were Southerners and went with the South. It was necessary for Lincoln to choose new generals to lead the immense new armies the North was raising, and with this important matter Congress constantly interfered.

It is hard to understand now, but politicians in

Congress in those days believed that they could command an army better than the professional soldiers. Others didn't want to be generals themselves, yet had no doubt that they were better than Lincoln at choosing generals. Certain Congressmen had pet officers, captains, majors, or colonels, who would, in the opinion of the Congressmen, make better generals than the men Lincoln picked, and if their pets were not chosen, these members would make trouble in Congress.

Kipling's famous poem *If* about what makes a real man begins:

> If you can keep your head when all about you
> Are losing theirs and blaming it on you,

and that describes Abraham Lincoln exactly. In the midst of men so excited that they acted like lunatics, he kept his head, and that is one of the main reasons why the North finally won the war.

Lincoln was man enough to keep most of the power of the Presidency in his own hands in spite of Congress. But there was only one Lincoln. When he was murdered at the end of the war, Vice-President Andrew Johnson became President, and poor Johnson was not nearly strong enough to stand up against the ambitious men in Congress. They snatched one bit of power after another out of the President's hands, and in the end even denied him the right to choose his own Cabinet. All the same, he kicked out the Secretary of War, Stanton, who, Johnson thought, had been conspiring against him, and appointed General Grant in his place. For that the House of Representatives impeached the President.

The word *impeach* means *accuse,* and only the House of Representatives can formally accuse the President of acts that make him unfit to hold office. Anybody can accuse him informally, and some people always do, but that means nothing. However, when the House impeaches him, he must be tried, and the only court that can try him is the Senate. But if the President is convicted and removed, the Vice-President, who ordinarily presides over the Senate, will become President, and it is not thought fit that he should preside when the Senate sits as a court to try the President. The duty, therefore, is temporarily assigned to the Chief Justice. This means that the judiciary, as well as the legislative branch, takes part in a Presidential impeachment trial.

In President Johnson's case the impeachment failed by only one vote, and it failed largely because Chief Justice Chase, presiding, insisted on making the trial a perfectly fair one. The system of checks and balances had worked again, and the legislative had not taken over all the executive power.

But Congress had gone pretty far. Lincoln, the man who kept his head, thought that when the war was over, it was over, and ought not to be continued by other means. Therefore, he favored bringing the seceded States back into the Union as rapidly as possible, requiring only that they abolish slavery, and that at least ten per cent of their people take an oath to be loyal thereafter to the Union.

The leaders of Congress, however, were not Lincolns, and they had a different idea. They would not admit that the North had done anything to bring on the war, holding that it was entirely the work of the South and that the South, therefore, ought to be punished. With Lincoln out of the way, they did punish it. For a time, they abolished the eleven Southern States altogether, converting them into five military districts, each commanded by a general, and they kept them under an army of occupation for varying periods, ranging up to more than ten years.

This policy wrecked what little of the South the war had not already ruined, and created hatreds that have not entirely disappeared after nearly a hundred years. The effort of Congress to assume the powers of the Presidency nearly lost the war and did inflict great and long-lasting injury upon the country. Once again it was proved that the system of checks and balances was one of the wisest things the Founding Fathers invented.

When the impeachment of President Johnson failed, it was the end of the last bold effort of one branch of the government to seize powers plainly given to the others. It was not the end of conflict. There have been squabbles ever since, but most of them were over powers that the Constitution did not plainly allot to any one branch. When a direct conflict has arisen between two branches, it has been settled by an appeal to the people. For instance, during the Civil War Congress enacted an income tax, which was collected for nearly thirty years. In 1893 the Supreme Court suddenly declared that it had no right to levy such a tax. For a time Congress submitted, but in 1909 it appealed to the people. It submitted the Sixteenth Amendment, giving it the right to lay income taxes, and in 1913 the amendment was adopted.

Within the twentieth century there have been two great upheavals that have changed the nature of Congress and both were directed against powerful, but unpopular leadership within Congress. That in the House broke the power of the Speaker in 1910; that in the Senate resulted in the Seventeenth Amendment that took the election of Senators from the State legislatures and gave it to the people. Both reflected a revolt among the people against domination of the whole government by Big Business.

The Speaker of the House had always been regarded as a very important man, and such Speakers as Nathaniel Macon, Henry Clay, and James G. Blaine increased its prestige. In 1889, when Thomas B. Reed, of Maine, became Speaker, it reached the top. In 1890 the House adopted a new set of rules, "Reed's Rules," that gave the Speaker almost absolute power over the business of the House and won for him the sarcastic name of "Czar Reed." Reed, in fact, was not always bound even by his own rules; sometimes he made new ones as he went along.

The most famous case was when he broke up a neat little scheme of the opposition when it desired to delay proceedings. Someone demanded a roll call, and when the clerk read out the names the opposition members sat still. At the end someone made the point of no quorum and the roll, sure enough, showed that only twenty, say, had answered to their names. Reed simply instructed the clerk to mark as "present," a member who did not answer but was sitting there, in plain sight. The opposition raged, but the Czar made his ruling stick.

Then, after Reed, who died in 1903, came a picturesque character from Illinois, Joseph G. Cannon, a skinny type with chin whiskers like an old-time country farmer. More ruthless than Reed, but with a quaint sense of humor that made him much more popular, he was "Czar Cannon" to his enemies and "Uncle Joe" to his friends. But Uncle Joe went too far. When a young Representative from Nebraska named George W. Norris appeared in the House full of idealistic schemes that he wished to introduce, the Speaker quashed him mercilessly. It was a bad mistake, for Norris, who became a far greater man than Cannon in later years, organized the discon-

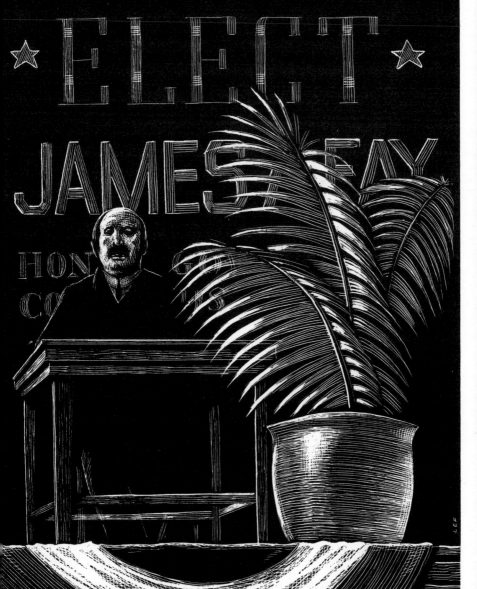

tented Republicans, combined with the Democrats, and shattered the Speaker's power by adopting a new set of rules.

This was in 1910, and the next year both houses submitted the Seventeenth Amendment, which was ratified in 1912. This was in part a revolt against a Senator who ruled the Senate much as Speaker Cannon ruled the House. He was Nelson W. Aldrich, of Rhode Island. But it was less a revolt within the Senate than response to a popular movement outside Congress. The flat truth was that too many rich men had been buying seats in the Senate by bribing members of State legislatures; or, what was even worse, great corporations had been buying seats for their yes men, who could be relied on to vote as the corporation wished, regardless of the good of the country.

Direct election of Senators by the people changed the nature of the Senate, some say not for the better. To be elected to the Senate today a man must have, first of all, ability to convince a majority of the people, including some ignorant and stupid ones, that he is able and honest. Some very fine men lack that ability and so can never be Senators, which is a loss to the country. While under the old system some men could buy their way into the Senate with money, under the new one some men can worm their way in by stirring up hatred and strife, by telling lies and inventing bogeymen to scare the stupid into voting for them. Is that sort of thing really any better than straight-out bribery?

In favor of the new system, however, two things can be said. First, it is not always true that whenever a fine man cannot be a Senator the country loses. Some very fine men ought not to be Senators. They are better fitted to do other things. Government is an art (or a craft, or a science — anyhow, a special kind of job) at which some highly intelligent men are just no good, while others, less brilliant, are very good indeed. Government deals with people, and men who haven't the knack of dealing with them ought to go into some other kind of work.

As for the second point, it is hard to deny that since Senators have been elected by the people, we have had some so crude that even a crooked legislature could hardly have been bribed to elect them. It is indeed a dreadful thing to see a United States Senator wasting his time denouncing people on account of their race, or religion, or calling everybody who shows any intelligence a Communist. It makes the country look ridiculous. Yet when a State is represented by one of these foolish fellows, the people of that State cannot excuse themselves by saying that the railroads, or the trusts, or the Money Devil of Wall Street put him there. The people put him there. The shame of it falls on them, and they cannot escape it. When they once realize how shamed they are by their Senator, they will learn to vote for better men. It is part of the process of learning how to govern ourselves.

Occasionally two branches of our government have joined to check the third branch on a question of policy. A famous instance occurred in 1937, when a large part of Congress joined the Supreme Court in resisting President Franklin D. Roosevelt's proposal to enlarge the Court from nine to fifteen members. There was no doubt that Congress had the power to do it. At various times the number of Justices had ranged from five to eleven by act of Congress, and there was no reason why the number should not be made fifteen if Congress saw fit. But many Congressmen felt that the proposal was an effort by the President to compel the Court to accept his ideas, and that they did not like.

It was a time of great economic distress, with

thousands of business houses failing and millions of people out of work. The President proposed, and Congress enacted law after law intended to relieve the distress, and time after time the Court, by a vote of five to four, declared those laws unconstitutional.

The President and his friends believed, and said loudly, that since four of the nine Justices agreed that the laws were constitutional it was certainly a matter of doubt. Therefore, they argued, the five were striking them down, not because they were unconstitutional, but because the five deemed them unwise, and it is not the function of the Court, but of Congress, to decide whether proposed laws are wise or unwise.

This was all very well but, on the other hand, if Congress gave the President six new Justices of his own choice, this would give him, since four were already voting with him, ten votes to five. Would not this be, in effect, allowing the President to tell the Court how it should decide cases? It was right and proper to stop the Court from trying to take over the lawmaking power, but it was equally right and proper to stop the President from taking over the judicial power.

What happened was that one of the five—some say

by persuasion of Chief Justice Hughes—suddenly
began to vote to hold the new laws constitutional.
This meant that instead of being struck down, the
acts of Congress were sustained by votes of five to
four. That gave Congress an excuse to reject the
President's proposal, which it did.

Who won that fight is still not clear. Friends of the
President, Congress, and the Court all claim the
victory, but a neutral may be inclined to think that
what really won was none of them, but the system
of checks and balances. The Court was discouraged
from trying to make law. The President was discouraged from trying to "pack" the Court. Congress
remained independent of both. That seems to have
been the outcome of the great Court fight of 1937.

Most of the recent great battles in Congress have
been fights to direct and control the power that Congress certainly has, rather than to acquire more. An
exception is what is known as "the Bricker amendment," so called because it was introduced by an
Ohio Senator named Bricker.

The Bricker amendment has never passed Congress, and the Senator himself disappeared from
Washington in 1956, but something like it is still
favored by many members. The idea is to restrict the

power of the President to deal with foreign nations. Under the Constitution the President sends and receives ambassadors, makes arrangements about such things as exchanging mail, agrees on the conditions under which ships shall enter and leave ports, and handles practically everything else that has to do with other countries, with two exceptions. Only Congress can declare war, and only the Senate can ratify a treaty to make it binding.

Some Senators have been much annoyed by this, because it leaves foreign affairs almost entirely out of their control, and they have grown more annoyed as foreign affairs have grown more and more important. A clever President, dealing with friendly nations, can get most of what he wants done without a formal treaty and, therefore, without the consent of the Senate. Senator Bricker proposed to amend the Constitution so that any kind of agreement with a foreign nation would need the consent of the Senate, just as a treaty must have it now.

The amendment never has been accepted, because the President needs much greater power over foreign affairs than he needed in 1787. When the only means of getting news fom Europe was by means of a ship that took three to six weeks to cross the Atlantic, there was ample time to discuss and consider, because nothing could be done instantly. But that is no longer true. Now that news travels around the world with a speed of light, many decisions must be made immediately, and a delay even of a few hours may make the decision too late.

We have to make a choice between two dangers. To leave important decisions to one man is dangerous, because we have found by experience that the combined wisdom of the whole country is greater than the wisdom of any one man. As the Bible says, "In the multitude of counsellors there is safety."

On the other hand, when the rest of the world is moving fast, there is danger in not being able to keep up. President Truman found that out in 1950, when the North Koreans came swarming across the dividing line without a moment's warning. He had to decide then and there whether to fight or to surrender. He fought. It is very difficult to keep up if you must call together a hundred men and let them argue it out before you can do anything. When something needs to be done immediately, to do nothing is always wrong. If you allow one man to act quickly, there is always danger that he may do the wrong thing, but there is a chance that he will be right. Doing nothing allows no chance of doing the right thing.

So far, the country has felt that it is less dangerous to leave matters in the hands of the President, who can act swiftly, than to tie up everything while we wait on a slow-moving Senate. That is why the Bricker amendment has been rejected up to the time this book was written. But this is no assurance that it will always be rejected. If some future President should make a series of bad mistakes in conducting foreign affairs, we might decide that it is safer to cut down his power.

Another conspicuous change has come in recent years to the Congress, not so much in its nature as in its relation to the country. It is the development of what is called the investigative process, which means the right of Congress to ask questions and demand truthful answers.

The right, it has always had. The way in which Congress uses the right, however, has undergone a great change. The Constitution, in giving Congress the right to make all laws necessary to accomplish the purposes of the Constitution, gave it the right to acquire the information upon which such laws must be based. That right has never been questioned. But gradually it came to be realized that mere publicity is a force of terrific power, so great that by it you can sometimes do things you could never accomplish by law. This realization was speeded in 1912 by an investigation of banking and the control of money under a committee headed by Representative Arsène Pujo, of Louisiana. The report of the Pujo Committee served as the basis of a law creating the Federal Reserve System, but by exposing the injustice of certain financial practices that the law did not touch, it also put an end to them.

It was speeded up again in 1924 when, largely through the efforts of one man, Senator Thomas J. Walsh, of Montana, Congress was pushed into an investigation of the acquisition by private companies of the Teapot Dome and other naval oil reserves. This investigation did not lead to much new law, but it did tear open a terrific scandal that culminated in sending a former Secretary of the Interior to prison for taking a bribe.

The Pujo investigation resulted in giving us a number of valuable new laws. The Walsh investigation resulted in cleaning much corruption out of government. But politicians took note that both had effects far beyond the legislation in one case and the prosecutions in the other. Here, plainly, was a new implement of government, one that could guide and direct the tremendous force of public opinion, which is often more powerful than law.

Therefore, the investigative process is being used more and more frequently, sometimes for purposes that are admirable, sometimes for others that are questionable. Everything depends upon the man conducting the investigation. If he is sincerely trying to get at the truth, and nothing but the truth, his investigation is always a good thing. Even if it shows that the charges are all nonsense, that there is in fact nothing to investigate, that is a good thing, because it exposes the liars who were trying to injure innocent people.

But if the man in charge really cares nothing about the truth, but hopes merely to embarrass the opposite party, or to destroy some personal enemy, or to gain a reputation for himself, the Congressional investigation can be turned into a weapon of frightful tyranny.

Article I, Section 6 of the Constitution says that for any words he may use on the floor of either house a member "shall not be questioned in any other

place." This means that he cannot be sued for slander or libel, or indicted for sedition, or punished in any other way except by the house of which he is a member. It is wise and necessary in order that members may be free to say what they believe to be true without fear of the revenge of some powerful person who may feel offended.

But is is a very different thing when a member charges some person with villainy, then conducts the investigation himself and will not allow the person accused to present his defense. A few years ago one Senator, Joseph McCarthy, of Wisconsin, became so notorious for that kind of thing that at last the Senate itself had to censure him.

It was different, also, when the House set up a standing committee, not a special committee, with the vague title of Un-American Activities. Its function is to investigate incessantly something that has never been defined. What it is popularly supposed to do is to investigate sedition, but that, again, is a very vague idea. To an ardent partisan, any criticism of his party borders on sedition, although to ardent partisans on the other side it is patriotism. Congress has never yet enacted a law based on information discovered by the Un-American Activities Committee, but never doubt that it is powerful! For many years the mere fact that a man was investigated by this committee was enough to cost him his job, for it was extremely difficult for him to present any defense.

So the investigative process is regarded very doubtfully by many persons, although it has become one of the most important activities of Congress. Congress must know the facts before it can legislate wisely on any subject, and the only way to get the facts is to investigate. To that extent the process is absolutely necessary to good government. At the same time, it is a terrible weapon in the hands of insincere persons or fanatics, and can be made to serve the purposes of tyranny, which is very bad government indeed. The problem, then, is to work out means by which this new method of governing may be used for good ends and be prevented from being twisted into evil.

The perfect solution, of course, is plain enough. It is simply never to elect to Congress a man who is not fit to sit in Congress. But perfect solutions are never to be attained in this world. We may work toward them, and hopeful people believe that we are working toward this one, but it will be a long, long time before we come close to it. In the meantime, we must use such makeshifts as we can, and some of the ablest members of the present Congress are busy working on various schemes to make the investigative process somewhat more effective and somewhat less dangerous.

But they cannot do much without support from plain people who know what it is all about. Like every other problem of government, it always comes back at last to the people. In Congress the American people have a legislative branch that for our purpose of preserving liberty under law, is as good as any in the world, and a great deal better than some. But it is not perfect, and it will not be brought nearer to perfection simply by denouncing what we consider the wrongdoing of Congressmen.

For the men who are there were sent there by the American people, including you and me. If at times we are tempted to lose our tempers and call them poor specimens, let us stop and think of what that implies. If they are poor specimens, what about the people who picked them for the job?

If we are honest with ourselves, we will admit that Congress, however you look at it, is exactly what we asked for, and exactly what we deserve. The gloomy will say, that is dreadful. But the hopeful will think it not so bad. They will apply to Congress the words of a famous German, Karl Jaspers, and call it what he called the university, "one instance in the hazardous enterprise of freedom which the western world, so far the only civilization in the history of humanity to do so, has undertaken."

Speakers of the House of Representatives

Name	Party	Tenure
Frederick A. C. Muhlenberg	Federalist	1789-1791
Jonathan Trumbull	Federalist	1791-1793
Frederick A. C. Muhlenberg	Federalist	1793-1795
Jonathan Dayton	Federalist	1795-1799
Theodore Sedgwick	Federalist	1799-1801
Nathaniel Macon	Democratic-Republican	1801-1807
Joseph B. Varnum	Democratic-Republican	1807-1811
Henry Clay	Democratic-Republican	1811-1814
Langdon Cheves	Democratic-Republican	1814-1815
Henry Clay	Democratic-Republican	1815-1820
John W. Taylor	Democratic-Republican	1820-1821
Philip P. Barbour	Democratic-Republican	1821-1823
Henry Clay	Democratic-Republican	1823-1825
John W. Taylor	Democratic	1825-1827
Andrew Stevenson	Democratic	1827-1834
John Bell	Democratic	1834-1835
James K. Polk	Democratic	1835-1839
Robert M. T. Hunter	Democratic	1839-1841
John White	Whig	1841-1843
John W. Jones	Democratic	1843-1845
John W. Davis	Democratic	1845-1847
Robert C. Winthrop	Whig	1847-1849

Name	Party	Tenure
Howell Cobb	Democratic	1849-1851
Linn Boyd	Democratic	1851-1855
Nathaniel P. Banks	American	1856-1857
James L. Orr	Democratic	1857-1859
William Pennington	Republican	1860-1861
Galusha A. Grow	Republican	1861-1863
Schuyler Colfax	Republican	1863-1869
James G. Blaine	Republican	1869-1875
Michael C. Kerr	Democratic	1875-1876
Samuel J. Randall	Democratic	1876-1881
Joseph W. Keifer	Republican	1881-1883
John G. Carlisle	Democratic	1883-1889
Thomas B. Reed	Republican	1889-1891
Charles F. Crisp	Democratic	1891-1895
Thomas B. Reed	Republican	1895-1899
David B. Henderson	Republican	1899-1903
Joseph G. Cannon	Republican	1903-1911
Champ Clark	Democratic	1911-1919
Frederick H. Gillett	Republican	1919-1925
Nicholas Longworth	Republican	1925-1931
John N. Garner	Democratic	1931-1933
Henry T. Rainey	Democratic	1933-1935
Joseph W. Byrns	Democratic	1935-1936
William B. Bankhead	Democratic	1936-1940
Sam Rayburn	Democratic	1940-1947
Joseph W. Martin, Jr.	Republican	1947-1949
Sam Rayburn	Democratic	1949-1953
Joseph W. Martin, Jr.	Republican	1953-1955
Sam Rayburn	Democratic	1955-1961
John W. McCormack	Democratic	1961-

Vice-Presidents
of the United States

Name	Party	Term
John Adams	Federalist	1789-1797
Thomas Jefferson	Republican	1797-1801
Aaron Burr	Republican	1801-1805
George Clinton	Republican	1805-1813
Elbridge Gerry	Republican	1813-1817
Daniel D. Tompkins	Republican	1817-1825
John C. Calhoun	Republican	1825-1833
Martin Van Buren	Democratic	1833-1837
Richard M. Johnson	Democratic	1837-1841
John Tyler	Whig	1841-
George M. Dallas	Democratic	1845-1849
Millard Fillmore	Whig	1849-1850
William R. King	Democratic	1853-1857
John C. Beckinridge	Democratic	1857-1861
Hannibal Hamlin	Republican	1861-1865
Andrew Johnson	Democratic	1865-
Schuyler Colfax	Republican	1869-1873
Henry Wilson	Republican	1873-1877
William A. Wheeler	Republican	1877-1881

Name	Party	Term
Chester A. Arthur	Republican	1881-
Thomas A. Hendricks	Democratic	1885-1889
Levi P. Morton	Republican	1889-1893
Adlai E. Stevenson	Democratic	1893-1897
Garret A. Hobart	Republican	1897-1901
Theodore Roosevelt	Republican	1901-
Charles W. Fairbanks	Republican	1905-1909
James S. Sherman	Republican	1909-1913
Thomas R. Marshall	Democratic	1913-1921
Calvin Coolidge	Republican	1921-1923
Charles G. Dawes	Republican	1925-1929
Charles Curtis	Republican	1929-1933
John Nance Garner	Democratic	1933-1941
Henry Agard Wallace	Democratic	1941-1945
Harry S. Truman	Democratic	1945-
Alben W. Barkley	Democratic	1949-1953
Richard M. Nixon	Republican	1953-1961
Lyndon B. Johnson	Democratic	1961-

Standing Committees of the Senate

Standing Committees of the House of Representatives

Standing Committees of the Senate	Standing Committees of the House of Representatives
Aeronautical and Space Science	Agriculture
Agriculture and Forestry	Appropriations
Appropriations	Armed Services
Armed Services	Banking and Currency
Banking and Currency	District of Columbia
Commerce	Education and Labor
District of Columbia	Foreign Affairs
Finance	Government Operations
Foreign Relations	House Administration
Government Operations	Interior and Insular Affairs
Interior and Insular Affairs	Interstate and Foreign Commerce
Judiciary	Judiciary
Labor and Public Welfare	Merchant Marine and Fisheries
Post Office and Civil Service	Post Office and Civil Service
Public Works	Public Works
Rules and Adminstration	Rules
	Science and Astronautics
	Un-American Activities
	Veterans Affairs
	Ways and Means

Index

*Indicates illustrations

A

Adams, John, 66, 70, 74-79
Aldrich, Nelson W., 102
Antislavery amendments, 92
Armed Services Committee, 26
Articles of Confederation, 54

B

Banking and Currency Committee, 25
Beauregard, Pierre G., 93
Bills
    calendar of, 36
    introduction of, 36
    number of, 65
    voting on, 21, 22, 24
    writing of, 36
Blaine, James G., 98
Bricker amendment, 106-108

C

Calhoun, John C., 80-88
Cannon, Joseph G., 99, 102
Capitol, 13, 27, 58-59, 62
Census, 19
Checks and Balances, 68, 69, 70-117
Civil War, 87, 90*-91*, 92
Clay, Henry, 81, 82*-83*, 84-88
Committees
    hearings of, 22*-23*, 37-38
    kinds of, 24
Compromise of 1850, 88
Congress
    contempt of, 38
    definition of, 52

houses of, 18-20, 46-50
investigative powers of, 109-116
life of, 63
Congressional Districts, 32-35, 56-57
Connecticut, 55
Constitution, 28, 32, 43-44, 46-49, 67-68, 109
Article I, Section 6, 111, 114
ratification of, 52
Constitutional Convention, 54-56

D

Delaware, 56
Dred Scott, 89, 92

E

Eisenhower, Dwight David, 65
Electoral votes, 20

F

Federalist, The, 67
Federal Party, 75
Federal Reserve System, 110
Filibuster, 49-50
Fiscal year, 27
Franklin, Benjamin, 44, 52*-53*
French Revolution, 72*-73*, 74

G

Genêt, Edmond Charles, 74
George III, 74
Gerrymandering, 33-34*
Grant, Ulysses S., 95

H

Hamilton, Alexander, 52*-53*, 67, 71, 74-77
House Un-American Activities Committee, 114-115
Hughes, Charles Evans, 106

I

If, 94
Impeachment, 95-97
Income tax, 97-98
Interstate commerce, 67

J

Jackson, Andrew, 79-84
Jaspers, Karl, 117
Jay, John, 67
Jefferson, Thomas, 71, 74-77, 88
Johnson, Andrew, 94-98
Johnston, Albert S., 93
Johnston, Joseph E., 93
Joint committee, 24
Judiciary Act of 1789, 77

K

Kipling, Rudyard, 94

L

Law, 14-16
Lawmaking, 46
Lee, Robert E., 93
Legal residence, 28-29
Legislative, 14
L'Enfant, Pierre Charles, 57
Lincoln, Abraham, 66, 93-94, 96
Longstreet, James, 93
Lord Acton, 68

M

McCarthy, Joseph, 114
Macon, Nathaniel, 98
Madison, James, 44, 52*-53*
Majority leader, 49

Majority report, 28
Mandamus, 77
Marbury vs. Madison, 77, 79
Marshall, John, 77-79
Massachusetts, 55
Minority leader, 49
Minority report, 28

N

Naturalization, 28
Norris, George W., 99, 102
Nullification, 79-81, 84

O

Old Catawba, 33

P

Parliament, 18, 64, 78
Pennsylvania, 56
Perjury, 38
Pocket veto, 43
President, 38, 46-47, 54, 62-63
President *pro tempore*, 49
Pujo Committee, 110

R

"Reed's Rules," 98
Reed, Thomas B., 98-99
Representatives
    election of, 29, 32
    number of, 19-20
    qualifications for, 28
    term of, 29
    work of, 44-46
Rhode Island, 55-56, 102
Roman Republic, 59, 62
Roosevelt, Franklin D., 104-106
Roosevelt, Theodore, 40*-41*

S

Select committee, 24
 on Conduct of Civil War, 93
Senators
 election of, 29, 32, 102-104
 number of, 21
 qualifications for, 28
 term of, 29
"Seniority system," 26-27
Seventeenth Amendment, 102
Sixteenth Amendment, 98
Speaker of the House, 48-49, 62, 98
Standing committee, 24-25, 27, 39
Stanton, Edwin N., 95
State legislature, 34, 46, 102
Supreme Court
 Court-packing fight of 1937, 105-106
 judicial power of, 54
 Justices of, 38, 64

T

Taney, Roger B., 89, 92
Taxes, 46
Teapot Dome, 110
Truman, Harry S., 108

V

Veto, 42
Vice-President, 47-48
Virginia, 56

W

Walsh, Thomas J., 110
Washington D.C., history of, 57-59
Washington, George, 15, 44, 47, 52*-53*, 57, 65-66, 70
Washington Monument, 13
Webster, Daniel, 86-88
Wolfe, Thomas, 33